ANCHOR BOOKS

POETS FROM EASTERN ENGLAND

First published in Great Britain in 1995 by
ANCHOR BOOKS
1-2 Wainman Road, Woodston,
Peterborough, PE2 7BU

SB ISBN 1 85930 091 X

Foreword

Anchor Books is a small press, established in 1992, with the aim of promoting readable poetry to as wide an audience as possible.

We hope to establish an outlet for writers of poetry who may have struggled to see their work in print.

The poems presented here have been selected from many entries. Editing proved to be a difficult and daunting task and as the Editor, the final selection was mine.

The poems chosen represent a cross-section of styles and content. They have been sent from all over the world, written by young and old alike, united in the passion for writing poetry.

I trust this selection will delight and please the authors and all those who enjoy reading poetry.

Andrew Head
Editor

CONTENTS

HUMBERSIDE

Where old counties meet
The river seeps
Steel grey against
A cold clear sky.
Where flat fields greet
The sea so deep
And seagulls chase
The clouds that fly
Over boundaries old
And bridges new;
United now by taxes due.
A county, though soon to divide,
No more to be called Humberside.

Where fishermen cast
Their nets till fast
Full of silver
In an iron sea.
Where farmers toil
Against the soil
Cutting furrows
Beneath ancient trees.
Some industries new,
Others old;
Many becoming industries closed.
A county fighting to survive,
No more to be called Humberside.

Joanne Ramery

LITTLE THINGS?

They say those 'little things' mean a lot
Mean a lot? I'd rather say 'cost' a lot!
A beautiful diamond can cost the earth,
Platinum, gold, priced high in worth.
Pearls of rare beauty - truly a pleasure
Finest gift of your loves' measure!
Ornaments carved in ivory grand
Costing the animal realms of the land.
Finest furs worn by the rich
Looks better on the beast, instead of the bitch!
A day in the zoo - poor caged up birds
'Oooh - gorgeous creatures' are empty words.
Cute little bunnies dying in pain
In the name of the businessman and *his* gain.
Tea from the Indies must be alright?
Sure, if the workers could sleep safe at night.
Pure cotton on our bodies to wear
Picked by child labour, you don't even care!
We may pay in cash, we feel no dismay
Will owning these *little things* love display?
. . . 'Little Things Cost Too Much.'

Constance Yvonne Moss

AN UNPAID PERSON

We're sorry to say
You're life's been cancelled today,
Without any return or advances,

So, if you please, would you
Pay all respects to those due,
And resolve your debts and finances.

Oh dear, it's a shame,
But I've forgotten your name,
Please remind me of it in due course.

I'm afraid it's too late
We have closed the gate,
There is no return from here, as you see.

You failed to pay
Your respects the right way
That's why you're here, says our source.

You can't complain,
As it's going to rain.
What do you expect? You can't blame me,

I'm simply doing my job,
So please shut your mouth,
I am due home by half past three.

Gemma Knowles

THE RELEASE (7.12.94)

I am seen as a paragon of virtue!

I work in a hotel and in a shop.
When serving the public I am helpful and polite.
They compliment me on my cheerfulness -
They don't see me on a Saturday night.

At school, I study for three A-levels,
Weekdays and weeknights I read, learn, write.
The teachers say I'm clever and I'll get good grades -
They don't see me on a Saturday night.

In rehearsals I search for the motivation
So that I can show Salieri's plight.
The teacher says I'm *wonderful* and *a star* -
She hasn't seen me on a Saturday night.

I'm free, alive, running in the wind.
Although it's dark, my life is bright.
Singing, laughing, kissing, joking,
Thanks only to the alcohol on a Saturday night.

Joseph Lidster

SURGERY OF THE MIND

Sat in my chair, making no sense
Of the surgery of the mind
Looked up at the ghost in the corner
He looked the same as me
Tranquil and overdrawn, my whisper awoke him
But our eyes didn't meet just looked at his feet

He didn't speak and his mouth dropped low
My mind sailed away with his to be free
The spirit shook his shuddering shoulders
But he wouldn't speak to me

Defenceless and unable to move
His tiny eyes captivated the room
My hairs on my back had bottled out
Who had cut him loose from his tomb

Speak to me or leave this world
The overpowering justice of it all
Take with you your brand new soul
Capture it all

The surgery scars are showing
My minds focal point is blurred
I remember the people closing in
How I had been so scared

Let me ride with you a while
My time is nearly up
The children sing but no longer with us
Were all that's left behind

Alone again, I think in rhyme
Hard decisions lose their prime
I appeared to be cruel just to be kind
Stole the golden ritual from his mind.

Phil Dalton

REEDHAM GHOST SHIP

The wind was high and howling
And whistling through the mast,
As the ghostly Viking ship
Up the river did come past.

Aboard her creaking decks
Under cover of the shields,
There was a crew of Vikings
Eyes searching o'er the fields.

They are heading up to Reedham
On this dark and misty night,
Just outside the Lord Nelson pub
The King to find and fight.

Every year it's said to happen
This battle from the past,
Those with the sight to see it
Have been left quite aghast.

As soon as the ship
Strikes the land,
Out jumps the screaming
Viking band.

The King appears from nowhere
On a great white horse,
He is pulled off his mount
And murdered why of course.

When the fight is over
They go as if a mist,
Now will you tell me
That ghosts don't exist.

K A Hollis

NORFOLK, MY PLACE

City life, countryside, surrounded by green
Norfolk, my place, so much to be seen
Thinking of home when I'm far far away
My thoughts keep returning to you everyday

Norwich, so small but so friendly as well
Different from Sydney where I currently dwell
The Cathedral, the market, I know every street
Where there's always a friend I'm sure that I'll meet

Sydney is fine but it's not quite the same
So many people not knowing my name
Opera house, Castle, which do I prefer
I've enjoyed being here, but I couldn't defer

Tamzin Hardy

HIDE AND SEEK

I sought the blue sea when the sea-mists were flowing,
When the sea-mists were flowing and filling the creek;
I found only the blue of sea-lavender growing,
Spilling over the marshes where silver wings seek.

I sought when the west wind sent the mists flying,
Sent the mists flying high away from the sea:
Then I saw it resurging, heard it singing and sighing,
Flowing back to the marshes, reaching out to touch me.

E May Sumserali

CHANGING NORFOLK

Wide skies remain the canopy they always were
Vapour trails from military jets and civil aircraft
Flint fronted cottages, sturdy and true
Necklaced now behind chain-linked fencing
Windows draped with fancy ruched curtains
Gardens ablaze, flowers from the Garden Centre
No vegetables in kitchen gardens anymore.

Where are the real Norfolk natives?
Dialect lost or forgotten
Swamped by incomers
Anxious to experience unspoilt countryside,
Genuine village life, unlocked churches
And
Apples sold at the gate.

C M Porteus

THE PHEASANT

The whistleman is blowing a strange and chilling sound
cleft sticks raised high and waiting
now pound upon the ground
the bird never knew because nobody said
that the crisp sharp sound was the shot from a gun
and not to seek sanctuary near to the sun
Mrs P is fearful and Mr P looks proud
but beaters' feet are coming hard
on cold and frosted ground.

Crack a shot from a gentleman's gun
felled first bird, it flew to sun
so silent thudded to the ground
black gold streaks are sent to yield
rugged faced boys with sparkling eyes
eager now to hold the prize
to thrust it in their army sacks
and count the brace when they get back
Mrs P's dead silent, Mr P's not proud
the guns are coming closer still and death is all around.

How at the end of a murderous day
with the winter sun low in the sky
can Lords and their helpers toast birds they have killed
and all to make rich pheasant pie.

Zoe E Cromie

JUST A MEMO

I can't write poetry anymore
I've lost the knack
I've lost the score
My palette is broken
My brushes spent
But you gave me notice. . .
Before you went.

You found me disabled
From the attack by that man
You said you loved me enough,
And I believed you my man!
It took me fifteen years to find you
Since that torturous day
Why did you up and leave me
In such a callous way?

Christine

UNTITLED

Welcome, dear little Jesus
In my heart forever stay,
All my joy is your fulfilling
On my first communion day.

Forever old, forever new,
His gift himself, he gives to you
On this day so sweet and rare
His dear blessing, you to share.

I see you in that white robed band
Joyous by the altar stand
Heaven must surely seem always
Like your first communion day!

Peace and joy and love so strange
This lovely day will never change
Beauty and innocence you enshrine
In this sacrament of love divine.

May this day be bright and fair
Flowers and sunshine everywhere
God go with you along life's way
Remembering your first communion day.

Thoughts from your Prayer Partner on your
Happy day with much love.

Joan Greathead

UNWANTED

Nobody wants me, nobody cares
This is part of my fears
To be left here to be left there
But always to be put back into care.

It wasn't my doing, so they say why
I ran away
It was rejection from that day
What seems long ago, is now today
If only I could have someone to share
then I won't have a care.
I wish too that I could have peace of
mind, and find someone who's kind.

Aunties and Uncles will do just fine
for I know they haven't the time.
To be part of a family, just for a day
This I'm sure will let my fears go away
I don't mind a part-time mum and dad
In fact that would make me very glad
My life it seems has been so sad
What I really want is to be a happy lad.

Perhaps one day I can take a bow
and feel more proud as I do now
To have someone take me for myself
Not to be left alone on the shelf.

A mum and dad is what I need most
I hope I won't be left behind
For I need someone I can call mine
A lady like you would be divine
But people like you are hard to find.

I'll keep on waiting till it's my turn
And hope by then it won't be too late
The years it seems are passing me by
I'm too old now to cry
Please foster me - foster me now.

Kathleen Frost

MY FIRST EXPERIENCE OF BOMBING

An ancient peaceful city
Swathed in the warmth of summer:
Out of the sun silently
The raider shot -
A silver bullet -
Destruction his object.

The shrill whistling overhead
Instinctively made me dive for cover;
Petrified I lay on the floor
Eyes tightly shut.

The earth shivered with exploding bombs;
Smoke and dust rose mocking
The brilliance of the sunlight,
Making it unnatural.

The subdued chatter of neighbours
Brought me to my feet.

Later, oh so much later,
My father, zombie-like came down the hill,
A big man, dwarfed by horror,
Speechless, soot-black, dishevelled.
Never quite the same again.

Dorothy Mann

THASS A RUMMUN

They're funny folk in Norfolk
And talk a different way
They often say 'Mind how you go'
To pass the time of day
A Norfolk mile is further
Than any other kind
It's best to take a road map
For then your way you'll find
There's roads that go to nowhere
But if you ask the way -
They'll say that it's 'Just up the road -
Can't miss it! Lovely day'
Now if you come to Norfolk
Away from toil and strife
And make friends with a Norfolk man
You'll have a friend for life!

Maureen Lejeune

UNTITLED

'Very flat' quoth he
'Not so' say I
Open and undulating
A distant church spire
The evening ball of fire
A skylark sings out over the ripening corn.

'Rather dull' quoth he
'Not so' say I
Quiet and unhurried
A village event
Shopping mall and castle pageant
The sails shimmer over the inland seas
Leisure and pleasure
History and art
A city grand
Mighty forest and sovereign land
The bird call over dune and marsh.

'Too remote' quoth he
To some maybe
Living and changing
Our European family calls
To breech the walls and glowering sea
Citizens of the world stem from such as we.

M Yockney

IN PRAISE OF NORFOLK

Oh, to be in Norfolk, now that May is here.
It is the prettiest and tidiest time of year
The fields are all a-glowing in various shades of green
And every so often, golden rape may be seen.
The hedges now are neatly trimmed
But do beware a chilly wind.
We may seem cautious people, it often has been said,
But when you get to know us, forget what you have read.
Our stately homes are beautiful, a visit is a must,
So well kept and polished, owned by the National Trust.
Ever heard of Cromer crabs? Now is the time to buy some.
Fresh and tasty from the sea, they make a very nice high tea.
Yarmouth bloaters are well known and have a flavour all their own.
The North Sea laps upon our shores, sometimes it's happy,
                                       at times it roars.
Our roads are narrow so do not race
But if you must, Snetterton's the place.
We have a wealth of lovely churches, each village has its own;
The towers are mixed, some square, some steep, some round.
If inside you linger a sense of peace is found.
This is a Royal county, our dear Queen has her home
She will even let you in it, and around the grounds to roam.
Our Cathedral in Norwich is a gem
Built by some very clever men
It stands so tall against the sky
A joy to see when passing by.
If you want to be afloat, what better than to hire a boat?
Cruise on our Norfolk Broads and say,
'That really was a lovely day'.
Once you have been, you will return
And find you have a lot to learn.

Muriel Winn

THE END OF THE DAY

Blue melts into green and gold into orange
As the sun slips behind bales of hay
Now golden brown in the evening light and
The combines are all stored away.
Shimmering fragments still speckle the sea
As the last of the day trippers leave
Making their way back over the sands
Their homeward journeys they weave
Children's buckets full of treasures - picnic baskets empty
Small limbs now tired and aching
But faces full of glee.
The sea lavender changes colour as the light begins to fade -
In the silver water of the salt marsh
The last of the sea birds wade.
A curlew cries from somewhere near
Then all is quiet and still,
And silhouetted against the sky
The great black arms of the mill.

Jean Larner

ECHOES

Should you stand on Shipdam Base
When the hunters moon is high
Where nocturnal screech owls stalk and chase
The timid field mouse scampering by.

A night wind sings a sad refrain
Each plaintive note both sharp and clear
Beckons spectres from some dark domain
A phantom host of yesteryear.

Bold and bright beneath the moon
Behold the silver wraiths of men
Summoned by that eldrich tune
For one brief hour to live again.

Risen from their silent graves
In mildewed leather and flying clothes
Where they slumbered long beneath the waves
Or some forgotten dell 'neath vine and rose.

The watch towers shell of crumbling stone
Fills with wild and lurid light
While from the West there comes the drone
Of giant metal birds in flight.

Those long dead warriors raise their eyes
To vast and heavenly vaults serene
And a ghostly armada in the skies
Who are heard - but never seen.

Joseph Cope

MEET ME

My love meet me in space, in a corner of time
meet me in a vacuum a place that's yours and mine
meet for a little while with all the tinsel gone
meet me with love, while we have love, while still our lamp has shone.

Wrap me up in an old cloth and cover up my hair
take me to a barren room with nothing but a chair
sit me there upon it and face in front of me
and look deep into my eyes and see who you do see
reach into my being as reaching to my soul
and if you reach here and see her then see if she is whole.

Feel with me the loves, the needs the messages deep within
the waiting and the wanting the longing to begin
join with me for a little while in as spaceless space
share with me a little while your own true face
and if you have love for me, then share it for a while
I don't ask for forever just a space to love, to smile.

Ann Osborne

SERENITY

Norfolk is the county
Where I was born into
I'd walk along the country lanes
Enjoy the pleasant view.

The cows are grazing happily
In a meadow lush and green
Cart horses were a lovely sight
So rarely now are seen

Harvest for me was wonderful
Down to the fields I'd go
And watch the combine harvester
With picnic bag in tow

Please let us keep our countryside
As it was meant to be
With barns for owls to rest awhile
With hedges and the tree

So planners, please don't take away
The country we once knew
So everyone can come and share
The pleasant county too.

Ann Jones

STOPPING BY A COUNTRY CHURCH

Where umber light is softly crossed
By shadows aftermath
I gaze upon a fading tower
Beside my homeward path.

Standing still against the night
I see its shape anew
Realise the ancientry
Of hallowed ground and yew.

I cannot know how many times
A traveller passing by
Has seen this silent marriage -
Norfolk earth to Norfolk sky.

Alan Henderson

NORFOLK COUNTY

Re-live the age of old steam days, ride up beside the driver
                on the footplate of a standard gauge.
You will find that this joyride is all the rage.
Steam erupts with such power, the whistle blows
                which gives such pleasure,
Day long journeys filled with hours to treasure.
Nature reserves near Thetford Woodland and Mere for a fine day
Walking in the country away from the coast to Peddlars Way,
Windmills as in Holland, most have been restored, a most
                beautiful sight to see
Hear the wind whistle through the trees, see the windmill sails rotate,
                which fills with glee.
Fakenham races with all the excitement and the thrills of the race
Crowds gather and cheer when the winner finishes in first place
Places that look like tropical islands leisure pools
                great fun for family a tropical paradise.
This is the Splash North Norfolk, great leisure life
Tree lined pool terraces and a view of a great sunrise.
Visit Holt with the quaint shops, cafes and cobbled walk way.
With the sun shining over the hills, drive along the coastline
                and enjoy the sun's rays
This will be a holiday of a lifetime, with days to enjoy and remember
Even when the year ends and suddenly it's December.

Joyce Willis

NORFOLK MAGIC

There is something magic about Norfolk
            I feel I could write a book
There is something charming about Norfolk
            About every cranny and nook.

One can wander down a country lane
            And see some hidden treasure
Not material things of course
            But things which give one pleasure.

The little buds in Springtime
            Can be seen in every hedgerow
Wild flowers in the summer
            In every field and meadow.

In Autumn there is added bliss
            As nature shows her splendour
The colours are so magical
            The work of the great inventor.

Winter too has its special charm
            When Mother Nature takes a rest
One can still travel the country lanes
            Even winter will pass the test.

I'm glad I came to Norfolk
            Oh, so many years ago,
Its the sweetest place upon God's earth
            In sunshine, rain or snow.

Eileen Greenwood-Sadler

NORFOLK

A great expanse of cloud flecked sky
Merging with the wave creamed sea
And flocks of geese at the marshes' edge
Clear rivers lined with rush and sedge.

Wherries drifting down the Broads
Fields and woods of varied green.
Cottages of dark knapped flint
And gardens glow with every tint.

Walsingham and the Holy Mile
Norwich Cathedral and its spire.
Castle Mall with its new glass dome
Ancient and modern - it's my home.

Shirley Edwards

NORWICH

Enclave of centuries past
Whose turmoil has washed through
The fingers of time
Whose sentinels now whisper
Of grey squirrels and
Plump pigeons.
Walk through that archway
Into the shouts of traders,
The Osler and the Blacksmith
Swapping tales.
Sense the fear and anger
Of the mob as it rushed
To claim its rights
Of fair dealings;
Remember the stretched out debt
Of hunger and sickness.

This seeming cul-de-sac of time
Is just a pause
The space between
One heart beat and the next
Yet in such a space
Kingdoms rise and fall.

Geoff Gaskill

A LIFE MAPPED OUT IN NORWICH

A meek girl lived in Humbleyard.
She strolled round Pottergate.
Topography was her concern
connected with her fate.

The wind blew cold down Ice House Lane.
Her life was incomplete.
She sought a man in Gaffers' Court.
She starved in Opie Street.

She met her love on Unthank Road.
He lived near Strangers' Court.
They kissed on Liberator Road.
He was the play-boy sort.

They dined at nine on Lobster Lane,
at Grapes Hill both drank well.
On Hotblack Road he craved his way.
In Pudding Lane she fell.

She crossed White Woman Lane a bride.
He'd said he'd take her hand,
they'd live in bliss in Heartsease Lane
until they reached Tombland.

But on the way by Whiffler Road
she met him with his wife.
She threatened him down Thunder Lane,
on Gun Wharf took his life.

In Judges Walk she weighed the cost
of loving such a snake.
She knew her trip down Unthank Road
had been a grave mistake.

Jenny Morris

BARNHAM BROOM AIR

F one-elevens scare the sky-scape;
Roll, cloud-cracking, in their certainty.
Like Thor chasing the lesser Gods
From here to near eternity.
Borrowing our Barnham Broom air
To serve their war-round purpose.

And through that same village air
But keeping to the ground,
Car commuters, nine-hours city bound,
Desert their rural resting place,
Then, energies depleted,
Wheel back to sunset, supper and sleep,
Recharge and airily next day repeat
Furrowing our Barnham Broom air
To roundly etch their main life purpose.

And through that same village air
Grandads, fretting in their gardens,
Catch the sound of grand children's voices
Borne school-sourced along the Easterly wind.
Which artfully borrow our Barnham Broom air
To pose a restful roundness, as always was,
To nature's main life purpose.

Much used, our air in Barnham Broom
No longer serves a village end.
Except the Church bears witness still
To changing times and changing ways
And seals within neglected walls
Our emptied main-life purpose.

Derrick J Clavey

THE STORY OF BEAUTIFUL BACTON

I was but a tiny tot when I stared in wonder at a cottage small with rustic gate
o'er which climbed kitten fat. My heart was torn asunder as I
longed to live inside that place so dear which overlooked golden sand
and rolling tide.

Snow white curtains made of lace, the front door open wide,
through frame of honeysuckle pink a rocking chair I spied,
complete with knitting lady, grey hair curled up in a bun,
with darling many-wrinkled face to whom I longed to run
and ask, 'Please may I stay with you for just a little time,
to sit in flowered garden and pretend that it is mine?'

All through life I've dreamed and longed to have about me,
grey stone walls which overlook golden sand and rolling sea.
Alas, our dreams can't always be fully realised,
perhaps another deity prevents a thing most prized.
But I shall have a pebble wall built when time is mine,
and with what joy those little stones in pattern I'll align.

So I spend what time I have picking pebbles from the beach,
each one a stone of happiness as near my goal I reach.

When I am old with wrinkled face, if God allows me that,
I shall buy a rocking chair and of course a little cat.
Then as I sit to knit and gaze about me there
at beauteous little pebbles my eyes will shed a tear,
of thankfulness and happiness to the God who made things all,
the sea, the sand all living things, and pebbles for my wall.

When I see a little child I'll say, 'Please come to me',
and tell her of the glories of the sand and rolling sea.
Of tranquil days at Bacton with its warm and friendly folk,
and the wealth of happy memories those pebbles will evoke.

When I am old and feeble, with no one else to care,
Then I'll talk to my pebbles and hope that they will share,
their memories of beauty in lands beyond the sea,
from where they could have drifted, and happy I shall be. . .

Madge Paul

SPACE

Poppies prance along hedgerows- seeds abandoned
By wind as it sweeps over wheat
Simple and honest they flower unashamed
Amongst rows of dark green sugar beet.

Down winter lanes the huge lorries fly
Taking rhizomes quite huge to transform
Into pure crystal sugar for making plum-pie
From the fruit on the trees-still summer warm.

The forest of Thetford, the Broads for a sail
The beaches for children and holiday camps
A stroll on the pier - fish over the rail
Not always hot - out come the gay gamps.

Cottages, mansions and council estates
Live check by jowl down the street
Pretensions are foreign to Norfolk's inmates
Pubs which remain are where they all meet.

Visitors marvel at that extraordinary light
Unshadowed by mountains or hills
To see cornfields rippling is a brilliant sight
A cure for all ills-far better than pills.

Some come here for health-some come for love
Which grows slowly and surely and true
Woven into her pattern-snug like a kid glove
You are honoured-one of the rare chosen few.

Shirley Hayward

SHERINGHAM RAILWAY

I could have been back in the olden days
old and battered though no windows shattered
rusty and dull but still people chattered.
Huddled in groups to keep out the cold, though
something 'stood-out' rigid and bold.
'The Writing', I thought, on the back of the train
something repeated again and again.
Though when I woke up, the same as before
but a different reflection in the old carriage door.

S Bemment

NORWICH CITY LIFE

Traffic here, traffic there
Roundabouts, thoroughfare
City lights, noisy nights
Artwork, markets, fruit delights
Castle mall, buildings tall
Musicians up against a wall.

Churches, pubs, library, banks
Queues of cars and taxi ranks
Coffee shops, lots of stores
People in and out of doors.
Who says that Norfolk is a bore -
This is the start, there is much more!

D Forrest

THIS NORWICH

High rise flats with splendid views to Mousehold and Cathedral spire
Whilst down below in city streets, cars of every shape and kind
fill the motorists' troubled mind,
No place to park you hear them cry;

In contrast to the streets below and tucked away from traffic flow
a chapel rests so silently, St Julian of Norwich.
This is the place that I love best, wherein the weary feet may rest
and so emerge with soul refreshed and ready for tomorrow.

This city steeped in history of ancient walls and cobbled streets
of market stalls and Castle Keep inspires the hearts of those who love
. . . This Norwich!

Vera Clouting

THE WINDING RIVER WENSUM

Oh gentle winding river your flowing waters have much to tell
Meandering through Norfolk's countryside has for centuries cast a spell,
A variety of marauders, and foreign invaders attracted to our coast,
In their boats from over the North Sea, along your banks new
                                        settlements to boast.

Roman legions, Anglo Saxons, Danes and proud Normans too
Rowed upon your waters from the coast, curious to explore and view
Landed by Tombland and settled, Norwich gradually did grow
An advantage point to build, as your timeless waters flowed.

Norman Bishop Herbert Losinga, nearly one thousand years ago
Came from France, a great Cathedral near your banks to bestow,
Left this earthly life before his work complete, but the die was cast,
Always on the horizon, its towering spire, a landmark to last.

Over centuries you have flowed gently, through your green lush valley
On into and across an historic, bustling, thriving city
From the North West of the county, and then outwards to the sea
Passing fine Churches, mansions, buildings, mills and factories.

You have witnessed heartbreak, plagues, pestilence and strife
Intermingled with rural trades, prosperity and invigorating life,
Resident proud achievers, resilient men and women
Their lives and talents to the city they have freely given.

A noble city sprang up around your twisting winding way
Has grown and flourished, its importance is well known today
Its ancient culture, and urban beauty is much admired and praised,
Completing the second millennium with heads proudly raised.

Oh peaceful winding Wensum you have seen it all,
Through countless ages, your gentle waters flow,
Gurgling along your merry way, are you unaware
Of all that's grown around you, as if you didn't care?

David Bunting

COUNTRY PICTURE

We sat beside the river and watched the boats go by
Just then we heard the cuckoo call from somewhere in the sky.
It was in early May time, sun shone, and gentle breeze
Caused leaves to rustle faintly in the nearby line of trees.
Not far away the cattle could be seen out on the marsh,
Then flew the great grey heron, with flight-call somewhat harsh.
The mallard resplendent - green head and purplish breast
Swam past us with his lady seeming suitably impressed.

It was so warm and pleasant, we could have stayed all day
The city's streets and shops seemed a million miles away!
But no, 'twas time to go again - pick up our trusty steeds,
To leave behind the water and twitterings in the reeds.

A E Collins

LITANY FOR NORTH NORFOLK

From a too easy acceptance of infinite skies
Stained windows of dusk, flamboyant sunrise
And the wind-glass lilting of larks, with heaven in their eyes
      Good Lord, deliver us.

From roaring waters overwhelming in the black night
From surging shock and terror, and a forced flight
From chill desolation in the grey creeping light
      Good Lord, deliver us.

From indifference to loud lamentations of summer night seas
To a suffering landscape of wind-tormented trees,
And heart-twisting limitless acres of lavender in the salt breeze
      Good Lord, deliver us.

Lord, let us hear each cry of the arrowing plover
Clear and true, as if life were nearly over,
And gather into the halls of our memory
There to drift in our dreams through eternity
Pebble and spume, sea-thrift, and seagull soaring
Slumbering moonlit deeps and the great tides roaring;
      Lord have mercy on us, and hear our prayer.

M W Andrews

THE POND

The pond I saw as a child is gone
the memory very clear lingers,
brought back to life by sound
a smell, sight of a flower,
Hazel leaves cold, touch my face
shafts of sunlight close my eyes
I smile.
the pond I saw as a child is gone
as I walk the torn up railway lines,
follow the stained corn paths
I can only just hear the sound of
the lawnmower in the distance,
the red and white lighthouse seems
to walk around,
plays hide and seek behind the trees
the pond I saw as a child is gone,
I stand at the abbey, stare across
the marsh, my mind visits the past,
voices cry out, boats sail and chug
by, plastic bottles bob up and down
gold red packets fly like birds,
choco this, choco that, all escaped
from boxes in the tidy shops,
the pond I saw as a child is gone,
please don't make me wear one of
your funny hats and live in a virtual
reality machine,
the child is gone.

I L Pegnall

SHERINGHAM

The waves that on the beach do play
Among the pebbles, white and grey,
I reach to touch - to place my hand
On pebbles moist, yet warm - on sand.

Summer, clothed in bright array
Beckons, invites, calls to play
And when the sun goes down - I stay
my feet on pebbles, white and grey.

D M Stone

DAYDREAMS OF NORFOLK

Wake up from your dreaming dear springtime,
And stretch wide your soft gentle hands,
Spread warmth over all of the beaches,
So the children will play on the sands.

There are ripples upon the clear water
As the mallards and swans have a swim,
Way below the tall reeds of the river,
There are flashes of silvery fins.

Too soon, the peace if now broken
By the roar of a great many boats,
As man pursues nautical pleasures,
There's a smell of strong fumes that can choke.

Like sentries the windmills stand lonely,
On grassland, without any sails,
Long gone is their reason for being,
Used hard by the winds they look pale.

For the farmers it's time to start reaping,
Their harvest of gold every day,
The long summer days are soon over,
And autumn is well on the way.

Again, now a soft breeze is rippling,
Across the great sea of tall grass,
The movement is flowing and gentle
Like the spirits of life from the past.

The thin icy fingers of winter,
Bring a stillness and quiet all around,
There's a hush of a world that is sleeping,
You see not a ripple, nor hear not a sound.

Brenda Rose Firth

MY NORFOLK

I've travelled North, I've travelled South, I've travelled East and West
But Norfolk always draw me back, that's the place I love the best
For here's the lovely scenic Broads, to leisurely sail around,
To see nature at its very best, birds and flora there abound.

The windmills proudly standing, as they've stood for many a year
Their working days now over, but their magic is still there.
Cattle, sheep and ponies, graze along the water's edge
Oldie pubs with fine cuisine, their friendly service pledge.

I take in all the beauty of town and countryside
Historic Norwich City with its Castle, and Cathedral high and wide
The royal estate at Sandringham, coastal resorts that are a gem,
All make the Norfolk that I love and I'm so very proud of them.

Mabel Weavers

THE LADYBIRD

Bishy, Bishy Barnabee, who painted your red cape
And clothed you in a waistcoat to fit your funny shape?
Of all Earth's tiny creatures you are truly blessed
With bringing news of summer joy and every happiness.

And when you are so busy in our gardens flush and green
Your little coat of colour can so easily be seen;
With black head a'bobbin and tiny feet so small,
You clamber thro' the briars and up the garden wall.

Chasing all the green-fly and cleaning flowers' leaves
Helping the busy gardener with his everyday needs.
Not seeking praise or thank you for all the busy chores,
You work away so busily obeying nature's laws.

And when the day is ended and your bed is calling nigh,
You take off your black collar with its dainty little tie
And cuddle up into a ball beneath a leafy bower,
To keep you snug and warm from April's sudden shower.

Michael Moore

HOTELS

Way back in 1933
A conference was held right by the sea
My grandfather who lived in Kent
He had to go, so off he went.

My grandmother, well she went too
And walked around to see the view
Great Yarmouth was this seaside town
She strolled all round, went up and down.

She found an Hotel up for sale
'I'd like to buy it without fail'.
And so she hold her husband Bob
'We'll move up here and start a job'.

They bought the place and moved from Kent
Opened it up, it was money well spent
They found another place to buy
And told their daughter to give it a try.

Their three sons decided to open Hotels
And so did the aunts and uncles as well
All the family ended up here
Working away throughout the year.

A dynasty - it had been born
They worked so hard from night till morn
Guests returned year after year
To breathe fresh air, they loved it here.

The family business it lasted for years
Right up to the nineties, but now though I fear
There's one Hotel left, the others were sold
The children went after their own pot of gold.

So, what happened way back in old '33
Allows me to live at this town by the sea.

Valerie Tuttle

THE OLD MILL

A tiny stream
Trickles by the old mill
Its sails were now very still
It was such a shame
They had not turned for years
Remembered by lots of folk
Who used to take wheat to be ground there
As years went by, the old mill
Took the strain of gales and rain
Its paintwork was the worse for wear
Sails were broken, it really was in a bad
State and needed urgent repair
One day this was to change
It caught the eye of folks that care
Now it has a coat of paint and
Brickwork all intact.
In fact it's looking great.
Folks can now see the sails turning in the wind
They stand and stare with great delight
The tiny stream now clear of weed.
A pathway round with palings painted white
A garden around the base
Flowers in full bloom
Such a lovely sight.

O Fuller

LARMENS FEN - SOUTHERY

Flat black landscape stretching away for miles
Odd trees dotted here and there like hairs on
a balding head.
Now and then a farmhouse stands isolated
alone and quiet
Like a solitary gravestone in the churchyard
of the dead.
We farmed in this lonely fenland world,
Surviving all of Mother Nature's scorn.
The strong March winds that blew away the
sugar beet seed,
Like husks from ears of corn.
Scorching, dry, relentless summer heat
When the earth cracked and split like old
dry skin.
And winters when dykes and rivers froze over,
With deep snow that blocked us in
Through all of this we worked the land,
From childhood we became young men
And looking back now from middle age,
With fondness I remember Larmens Fen.

Colin Leet

NORFOLK - A RAINBOW OF COLOURS

I see Norfolk like a rainbow
From rising sun thru into moonglow
Cottages, grey, flint so old
Poppies red in cornfields gold
Grass green hills, sandy knolls
Coloured shingle, under white waves, roll
Sparkling gems amongst the stones
Agate and amber are the ones -
Which I keep searching for,
Along the miles of golden shore.

Deep blue sea or green or grey
Changing colour, every day
Wide, clear skies of every hue
Scented land of lavender blue.
Dark brown earth beneath the plough
Autumn leaves of orange glow.
Sun rising from a gilded sea
Never fails to enrapture me -
And then to see it set the same
In purple shades and fiery flame.

The sea a path of molten gold,
Even in the winters cold.
Indigo nights with violet gleam
Diamond stars and bright moonbeams
Yes, Norfolk always seems to glow
With the colours
Of a rainbow!

K Lee

IN PRAISE OF NORFOLK

There's the North Norfolk coast that gave us Nelson
And the sailor lads who followed him to sea,
You can feel up there the air is 'different',
Like a wine that gives one strength, and it's all free!

On the Queen's estate at Sandringham in late Spring,
See the rhododendrons blooms, it's perfect bliss,
One can stand there in awe and admiration,
And think that heaven's no lovelier than this.

The Broads also has gently flowing rivers,
Where motor craft, or yachts sail in the breeze,
With picturesque towns and homely villages,
With their ancient pubs that nestle 'neath the trees.

The trees of Thetford forest have a beauty,
An aura of serenity and peace,
Yet till nineteen twenty two it was a warren
A sandy waste, where rabbits ran and squeaked.

In the South-West, black fens dominate the landscape
Farms dot the land as far as the eye can see
And the men who work these wild and lonely acres
They're the salt of the earth I'm sure you will agree.

Over six hundred and fifty ancient churches
Grace villages, some with ponds or streams,
With their different styles of mellowed old world houses,
Standing by themselves, or grouped round a green.

We have such different varieties of scenery -
When I'm taken around, I feel such pride
And affection for my beloved county,
And I pray my lovely Norfolk never dies.

Elsie Bowden

THE VILLAGE STORE

The corner shop, the village store
Some people say 'Soon be no more',
But in this time of rush and tear,
I'm glad our village shop is there.
No hustle, bustle, check out queues
But chatty gossip, village news,
Pensions given, stamps and post,
Denver shop has more than most,
Cottons, laces, elastic bands
Sherbet lemons, all at hand
Birthday cards, penny chews,
Household names that we all use
Best cooked ham, 'two slices please'
Free range books, pound of cheese.
Evening snack at five to nine
Village stores, just in time!
Orders taken - deliveries made
TV licence, phone bill paid
Each superstore should have its place
Stressing out the human race
For family shop it is ideal
Piled up trolley, wonky wheel
But give a thought for village life
Support the shop, help it survive
All this and more the stores provide
Don't say. . . 'The village shop has died.'

Cherie Woods

THE QUESTION

'Do you love me', you said and I
was taken aback
At the loss of communication
between us.
Arms swinging by your side, grey eyes
looking into mine. I pondered
at all the fuss
Grown-ups make of this question,
causing eruptions and wars;
But you, with your simple grace
looked up and said
'Do you love me? Because
If you don't I would
be sad, and cry -
Oh, child of mine - so
sweet and gentle, why
Do you have to ask?
I would give my life for you
Try to lead you through
this life of pain.
Do not my actions and
my words explain
You are my world, my all
I surround you with my care,
But with that innocent sweetness
All you do is stand and stare
And say. . . 'Do you love me?'

Peggy Briston

WE NEVER DID SAY GOODBYE

We never did say goodbye
I very often asked myself why
But goodbye is for ever
Forget you we could never
You where always there when we needed you so
You hated saying goodbye, you always liked saying hello
The nurses said you where a darling
They took you away without warning
We know the pain you hid
It did not matter what we did
We couldn't give you a pill
Because we know you where so ill
The angels took pity from up above
And carried you gently with their love
You were put into the Lord's care
Your heart of gold was very rare
He closed your eyes so you could rest
Because mum dear you deserved the very best

Catherine Thomas

GOLDEN YEARS

The days have gone when I could run
Along fine sands of gold,
And climb the tallest tree in town -
Such memories I enfold.

I see again a laughing child,
Unruly long fair hair,
And teddies, dolls and dancing shoes,
Two parents who did care.

The very special friendships that
I made along the way,
The presence of our loving pets
Brought joy to every day.

A toybox filled with magic things
Gave hours of pure delight,
And I remember too the thrill
It was to fly my kite.

Enjoyment of school holidays -
The freedom and the fun;
The mischief I got up to though
Was not enjoyed by mum!

Ambitions for the future changed
From one thing to another;
Yet little did I know how soon
I'd be a wife and mother!

The golden years of childhood passed
So swiftly out of sight,
Yet in my heart their glow remains
To shed my life with light.

Briony Lill

THE SYSTEM

Even colder on the inside, the unchained bound
The loneliness echoes, the only sound
Full lives lived on empty time. . .
Baron corridors, Graffiti Walls
Politicians decorate the
Empty halls.

Houses bought and dignity sold
Is this how we
Treat the aged and the old?
Its colder even on the inside
Lost souls, torn pride
Frozen lives, hours slowly
thaw,
And down the drain,
they disappear
and
are forgotten again
Outside it's cold and pouring rain
Is this our system?
How insane!

Fiona Collins

BOSTON MARKET

Boston Market has a special touch,
So long established, but it doesn't alter much.
The clanging of bars as the stalls are set up,
Lay out the display, time for a warm cup.
In winter with gales and storms and rain
We sometimes wonder if we are insane.
Hang on to your stalls, the wind whips the sheets,
Some of the stock rolling down the street.
But encircling the market with a solid façade
Old streets and buildings so long standing guard.

On Wednesdays in summer, day visitors come,
It's busy, exciting, the place fairly hums.
Some search for the bargains, some even haggle,
Groups of women go round in a gaggle.
The people are varied, as are the goods too,
And it's been like that for centuries through.
The metal bars clatter as they're packed away
And herald the end of the market day.
But above the bustle, timeless and serene,
The majestic tower of the 'Stump' can be seen.

Sally Quinn

LOCKED UNDER DREAMLESS SKIES

Our lives are but waves
Of which we are its slaves
Below the waves are the fish
These are the dreams of which we wish
Above the waves are the mocking gulls
They dive and snatch
These dreams of which we hope to catch
They take all our dreams until
None are left
Except the dreams of death, death, death.

Peter Lowe

A LINCOLNSHIRE LASS

Lincolnshire yields pastures and fields
Farming and growing, sheep and shearing
Toilers and tractors the strong men do wield.
Churches and steeples for the god-fearing.

Tulips abound in fields all ablaze,
Yearly there is a flower parade,
Chariots of colour parade through the streets
The young and the old unite to greet.

Long country lanes twist and wind on your way
Away from the roar of the big motorway,
The Lincolnshire lanes have managed to be
A haven of peace and tranquillity.

Towns are spread all over the shire
Mixed in between are the hamlets and spires.
Although there is change they still manage to show
What it must have been like years ago.

I come from Grantham a 'Yellow Belly' you know
There's nowhere else that I'd rather go,
A happier person I could not be
Living in a Lincolnshire county.

Fancy a seaside holiday swim?
Then go to Skegness and dive straight in.
It's only a short bus or car drive along
Our Lincolnshire Costa-Del-Sol.

I'm a Lincolnshire lassie, a bit old in the tooth
No doubt many would say a silly old boot,
But never the less I'm happy to be
A Lincolnshire lass of nearly sixty.

M Shelbourne

SITTING ON THE SEA WALL

Sitting on the sea wall
I'll tell you what I see
Looking out way in front
The mighty bold North Sea.

Sitting on the Sea Wall
I'll tell you what I see
To my left and to my right
Groynes point up at me.

Sitting on the Sea Wall
I'll tell you what I see
One side there are sand dunes
A kite flies in the breeze.

Sitting on the Sea Wall
I'll tell you what I see
The other side is houses
Homes for families.

Sitting on the Sea Wall
I'll tell you what I see
Down below the golden sands
Where folks bathe happily.

Sitting on the Sea Wall
I'll tell you what I see
Up above the clear blue sky
The sun shines down on me.

Sitting on the Sea Wall
I'll tell you what I see
My arms, my legs, my body,
Just sitting lazily.

Pamela Simms

CHAIN OF PEACE

If a flower would grow in a meadow
For everyone that said -
'Make this earth, a peaceful earth',
Then a ring of flowers would spread
Across the seas and around the world
With a scent that empowered all men
To take away pain and sadness
And bring peace to the earth again.

Glenda Anderson

SPRING

The springtime garden looks a treat
With primroses and bulbs so neat
I realise that April's here
And birds arrive from far and near
They love to peck at new green leaves.
Then carry food up to the eaves
A nest appears in drain or gutter
Small nestlings wait for 'bread and butter'.
I hope and pray that puss, next door
Will stay at home - not go to war!
Blossoms on the trees appear.
An early shower starts to clear.
The sun comes out and warms the ground
Small seedlings shoot without a sound
It's time to plant potato seed
I have a family too, to feed
Green peas and kidney beans as well
All go to make a garden 'swell'
Spring's a lovely time of year
Flowers to smell, birds to hear.

C Maltson

MY VERY LAST HOME

Now I'm a camper
a boy scout
out
on this wasteland
of cold unfeeling concrete
Here I lie and listen to the rain
playing a hollow tune
on the sea of scattered pools
tap dancing empty memories
on the paves of the old avenue
and all I wanted was you
to tell me what a fool
I had been.

I shouted out aloud
put my life savings
in this elusive Ideal Home
bricks and mortar
turning to a disaster
of investment in crumbling stone
I miss my wife
my family and kids
I miss my dog
I miss my once unyielding resolve
as I see a cardboard box
sag, fail and finally dissolve
until I loose my very last home.

M Ainsworth

LINCOLNSHIRE - HARVEST TIME - 1943

The stubbles high and spikes the shins
When trousers are far too short
Held up by binder twine and safety pins
- Or nails of any sort!

Jack has spats and belted coat
To keep out the morning cold
Flat cap and muffled throat
- And a horse that takes 'good hold'.

It's harvest time we fetch the wheat
From fields a long way off
The sun's well up and full of heat
Loaded wagon renews - Ned's cough

The war is on and we need the grain
To save us all from hunger
Work all day - ignore the pain
- Good bread a little longer.

The corn's now in a great big stack
As shapely as a loaf.
Made by Bill and our Old Jack
- Still laughing like an oaf!

Dry throats are slaked by flat brown beers
An eighteen hour day is ended
Men wander off to find their dears
- Their winding paths now wended.

The moon peeps o'er the boss's barn
A midsummer night at peace
God keep us safe on this old farm
- And let this war now cease.

J G Matthews

THE SEA

From deepest blue to eau de nil
Just depending on what mood it's in
As the tide flows in and out
A constant turning roundabout.

The lighthouse flashing through the mist
Spells out a warning to the ships
The beachcomber on his dawn patrol
Spies something lost from some poor soul.

The madly pounding giant waves
Relentless crashing near the caves
A sailors desperate cry for help
Is lost like countless tons of wealth

It gently laps the golden sand
As lovers stroll by hand in hand
The roundabouts and children's swings
Mingle with debris that it brings

The wondrous creatures of the deep
Keep swimming on - no time for sleep
The fisherman all tired and worn
Pray for calmness with the dawn.

Like a wild unchained beast
Or a kitten playing at your feet
The seagulls madly weave and dive
A daily fight just to survive.

As seaweed mixes with the sand
It covers most of all our land
It brings us wealth and food and warmth
A mighty power to thrill us all.

Heather Bowness

IT'S TOO LATE TO SAY SORRY

We had an argument one day, long, long ago
It's been so long - what it was about, I will never know
But watching someone close to us suffering each day
It's time the old wounds were healed up and sent along there way
I've heard a lot of people say this is the life they've led,
But brother it's too late to say sorry when one of us is dead.
So let's forget the fighting, feuding and the wars
Let's heal up the old wounds and settle all old scores.
Know matter who was right or wrong let it be said
It's too late to say sorry when one of us is dead
No doubt we'll have our off days and one or two small rows
But we won't make the same mistake by saying that we vow,
Never to speak to each other, we'll pass and turn our heads
But it's much too late to say sorry when one of us is dead
So let's wave the white flag and shake each other's hands,
And let's walk the future road with new interesting plans
Let's be the family that we were and let it again be said,
It's too late to say sorry when one of us is dead.

Margaret Hooten

MEDUSA

I am like the devils advocate
I only annihilate the good,
Evil I seduce,
But like everything else I cry.
I have held my tongue in your blood
For so long, I have become mute.
Red to red, red to death.
I have sacrificed everything to a God who may be dead
But I am learning to kill.
I believe in no religion, only my own way of life.
Husband I have eaten you,
My children, set free.
But I am still human like everything else.
Threaten me with hell.
Oh, I am daughter of Lucifer,
I grow breasts, I have a head, a body.
Do you see me as a dying orchid, crawling with maggots?
No mother, no father,
I am still your daughter,
Yet I have become hard and numb with wear.
Look, all you men
You have mopped up my tears with lies.
I devour men; I taint their blood with hate
And with my claws, I tear away their hearts.
And now, all I ask of you, all I ask of you,
Peel away the wax from my naked body
And you will find a woman
And I woman, and I woman,
Burn as a demon should,
And hang over this world, like a scarlet fever.

Rachela Colosi

DIFFICULT TIMES

Sometimes life seems so unfair
And pain is difficult to bear
But time does heal, and we grow strong
Recovering ourselves before too long
There's no sense dwelling on the past
Let it go, as life goes by so fast
Accept that life can get quite tough
And even when you've had enough -
Pick yourself up, put a smile on your face
Get through the crisis at a steady pace.
We often look back and don't understand,
But fate may deal us a winning hand.
Believe in yourself, and others will too
It's really not that hard to do
No matter how difficult, never to give in
Draw from the strength that is deep within
Life is for living so give it your best
Enjoy the good times, walk away from the rest.

A C Rose

MAN'S GREED

Be at one with nature, a balance should be kept
No more wide and deep trawling in the fishing net
The creatures of the ocean also need to feed
Stocks are now so low, with man's greed, greed, greed.

Timber from the forest felled indiscriminately
Habitat destroyed, animals killed, or flee
Wood adorns our houses it satisfies our need
But at the price for others, in man's greed, greed, greed.

Destroyed are the hedgerows where the birds would nest
Insects that pollinate no longer buzz, fly or rest
Concrete jungles thrive, where will all this lead,
We seem to always be on the take, in man's greed, greed, greed.

Natural springs of water, now polluted bitter taste
Chemicals hidden beneath beauty spots, deadly toxic waste
Children gasp for fresh air, a natural daily need
This is their inheritance, left by man's greed, greed, greed.

A Pendrous

BAND OF GOLD

I had a cry the day I sold
My only ring, my band of gold
Sometimes I think it isn't fair
When I look at my finger bare
Never mind it's just for show
In my heart I'll always know
For thirty years it's worn a groove
I have a band all pink and smooth.

Evelyn Ingram

YOUR ETERNITY

You cannot feel the laughter until you have shed the tears
Embrace the known without confronting the fears
You can no more taste the wine until you've drank the water
Enjoy the peace unless you've witnessed the slaughter.
You cannot go to heaven unless you understand the hell
Employ the good against evil to halt the rising swell
You can no more be alive unless you have been dead
Explain the ignorance then over beliefs we have been fed
You cannot give the answers to the questions that are asked
Enlisting the faithful to shield the masked
You can no more see a vision with more truth than mine
Expect then that 'Nothing' can be 'only' divine.

Jacqui Davies

LIVING IN SAFFRON WALDEN

Up here in this surrounded patch where does
Essex end, Cambridgeshire begin, Suffolk slide in
Hertfordshire harry the edges?
Voices blend and blur; North London
whine to true East Anglian undulation.

Can real Essex still be heard
or is all amalgam TV mish-mash?
Was that it in Great Sampford last
Good Friday? A whisper in the Co-op on
Tuesday market day, when villages converge,
bus borne, to visit, shop, in aisles stand
chatting.

Or will it, all too soon, submerge
be heard no more?
            Ah, yes.
For, toward May's end,
the Co-op closes.

Jennifer Coleman

ESSEX

Essex is an ancient place
And full of history;
There is so much of interest
But more than this to see.

Essex in the springtime with
New grass and violets blue,
Blackbirds singing in the lanes
And green shoots pushing through.

Essex in the summer and
The flowers are full of bees,
Cornfields ripening in the sun,
Cows seeking shady trees.

Essex in the autumn when
Woodland paths are gold and brown
With leaves and nuts and acorns
As they all come tumbling down.

Essex in the winter as
The seas crash on the sand -
North winds bring the ice and snow
To the sparkling frosty land.

Janet Swan

EYES

Look for eyes
that are smudged by history
shadowed by yesterday

Eyes that blink around the clock -
a mechanical savouring of dawn and dusk

Eyes wide and knowing
nothing of ignorance
A knowledge that comprehends
All things, but fact

Eyes that salivate
at the prospect of truth
Souring the grapes
of a fortified wine

Eyes that have lost
their way in the dark

Look for these eyes
and you too will be
All-Seeing
Un-knowing.

My eyes have been crucified
in this aftermath of incomprehension
A severed cipher/broken circle
Split and spitting venom
over intransigent verbs
and hieroglyphs.

Weeping without forgiveness

Jean Owen

PASSING COUNTRYSIDE

A patch-work quilt
Sage green, grey striped
Intermittent yellow and brown squares
Are edged, by a wall of stubble bricks
Cottages nestle in the sun
Lazily leaning on each other

A distant windmill with crossed arms
Surveys the scene.
Here a patch of brilliant blue
There billows of white
A pheasant struts in a moving hue
The green background enhancing it

J Skinner

EQUILIBRIUM

Rotating slowly with eternal devotion
turns the wheel of life in perpetual motion
For some more than generous with love to share
for others desperation, depression, despair.
Yet on counterbalance it's always on par,
for each short distance there is always a far.
For every new life born one will suffer a loss
for each suppressed underling a tyrannical boss.
Every bright light extinguished a new one re-lit
and each time you miss someone else has hit.
Each sigh of tedium heralds squeals of elation,
and for every single stranger a closer relation.
Tears shed through joy bring others through pain,
for each ray of sunshine there's droplets of rain.
Life is for the taking, but not without giving
take the good with the bad and you'll enjoy living.
For the wheel of life turns unbiased in action,
the outcome depends on individual reaction.
Rotating slowly with eternal devotion
turns the wheel of life in perpetual motion.

Julie Howard

OUR LOVED ONES

Outside the village but not far away
There is a field of green and grey
The grass is short some columns tall
The little church stands sentinel
All thru the ages it has seen pass by
Our wonderful loved ones who have gone to the sky.
With so much heartache and so many tears
Lovers have stood for many long years
Frightened and lonely they have lain to rest
All those dear ones we loved and blessed
But stay your tears, forget your grief
Some day the trumpeter will sound our name
Off we will fly to our loved ones arms again
To live for eternity on God's golden shore
And walk his gardens forever more.
- You and me!

Alfred Green

THINKING OF YOU

As you see the white of virgin snow
Which stops trees and flowers from growing
As children run and play the fool
I'll think of you.

As spring air starts to melt the snow
Blossom on the trees and flowers
Start to grow
I'll think of you.

As the summer sun rises high in the sky
Warm summer days and hot summer nights
As summer rain falls and the night slowly cools
I'll think of you

As autumn winds blow
And flowers no longer grow
Leaves on the trees turn golden brown
And fall to the ground without a sound
I'll think of you

As time goes by we start to see the
Path our lives have chosen to lead
And if our paths shall not meet
I'll think of you
When I close my eyes to sleep.

Michael Smith

DOVER AT NIGHT

The cry of a tormented lonely soul
The call of a seagull in the night
And my lost heart can't find its goal
So like the bird, it takes to flight
Its restless wanderings here and there
Give me no peace or time to spare.

Together we soar, we wheel and fly
Neither fettered by earth or sky
But after a time a bird must nest
While my poor heart still seeks its rest.
It wanders on through time and space
Desperately seeking a resting place.

But like the bird in the night
It's always ready to take to flight
One day maybe my heart will stay
Never more to fly away.

J M Bufton

THE CITY

The quiet street wears an orange glow
The shops are shut, windows dark and brooding
Like sightless, staring eyes
Long shadows dance and neon lights are harsh,
And crumpled rubbish blows through narrow alleyways.

It rains and filthy water rushes in the gutters
Sending cigarette packets bobbing and tumbling.
The last train leaves the station
A door bangs, a dog barks, then silence.
The city rests, it does not sleep for fear it might not waken.

D A Law

THE LOVE THAT ONCE WAS

You loved me; and so that day you asked me out
I had to say yes cos! I thought I loved you too
But then came the day I had to say it's over.
Then your friend came along and he loved me too,
Although it seemed that he did.
I messed it all up but I reckon
You too knew I was all confused
Now I'm left with no one.
It took me a while to realise
It was you, the one it should have been.
But now you're stuck in jealousy
Or is it just hate,
I know your love for me has all gone
And I'm left on my own to realise
What a stupid thing I done!

Clare Louise Jarrett

THE SOUND OF BELLS

From the old church tower so firm and square
the sound of bells comes clear through the air
as their rousing notes are carried wide
over houses, farms and the broad countryside.

With zest their craft the rope pullers ply
to spill out the peal from the belfry high
bell upon bell in fine sequence ringing
till the very stones themselves are singing.

From treble down to the great tenor bell
the dodges and changes are all going well.
The sallies dip with a wonderful feel
as clappers strike true the well cast steel.

In stately hall or plain village street,
in spreading field or small garden neat
near and far the people shall hear
the uplifting sound that quickens their ear.

And so the glad call once more goes forth
to west and east and south and north
for all good Christian women and men
to come together in prayer again.

Just as they did in that bygone age
when crinolines were all the rage
and grandfather's father was only a boy
the bells ring out still their message of joy.

David Poole

ABSENCE

I fear I have lost you to another
My oldest and dearest.
I fear I have lost you to candles and roses
Chocolates and glittering rings
And other gifts that lovers bring.
To the stolen kisses in the darkened back row
                of the picture house,
To the heady aromas of meadows in summer,
To the taste of good wine and fine food
To the sweet desserts
After.

Remember the days when we wished for love to happen
Our lives forever altered by the strength of another's passion.
But how great that alteration is
How damaging the passion
How quickly taken is my place by someone else's presence.
I cannot compete with the undefeated
That which first tempted then took
The emotion that basks in its triumph
My heart bleeds from the intense pain of loss.

Yet love will not take the past from me
I hold firm my sacred memories.
I reserve a space for the day to come
When it will bring you back to me.

Emma Lycett

NATURE'S MUSIC

The wind through the tall grass silently moves
Sending out sounds of whispering tunes
Reeds by the river join this haunting refrain
Gently swaying in time with the rain.

Leaves on the tree make a rustling sound
Like the gentle movement of a taffeta gown
The whistling wind through wooden fence blend
As flutists' notes heavenward send.

The patter of raindrops beating retreat
Steadily increasing the rhythm and beat
Thunder erupts like a percussion drum
A crashing crescendo of a bellowing gun.

Phyllis Smith

SUSIE

Susie was a slim brown dog
Her speed was second to none.

Her mistress she obeyed.

In a little village she did live beneath a great
big hill, where she would have her evening run.

When her mistress clapped her hands
To the top of the hill she ran.

The hillside moved beneath her feet with
rabbits everywhere.

Her mistress shouts and she returns
The rabbits saved for another day.

Susie sat by the garden gate
In late afternoon, for she knew that
the little children would pat her on the
head as they pass by.

Susie was a well loved dog
Alas! She is no more.

G F Snook

JOURNEY TO CLACTON

Opposite: the PR man - old but dark-haired
        And wrinkle free.
He's flirting with his secretary, or his lover,
        Or both.

To my left: a Spanish lady,
        Complete with guitar
And a bag, into which
        She must have packed her castanets.

To my right: another man,
        But much weaker than the first.
One look at him at him and you knew that he would
        Never succeed.

I wanted a window seat.
But, instead of a view,
All I got was a choice
Of different faces.
Each so important to its owner,
Yet only of minimal, passing interest
To me.

Levi Pay

LIFE IN THE FAST LANE

Stand still. Step back, and look around
With fresh, clear eyes at all you know
See the familiar anew
And wonder 'Was it always so?'

All round is rush and hurry
As life moves at a frantic pace
Cars, on roads like swollen rivers,
Are locked in an unheeding race.

Longer, wider roads we cry for
Which, when we get, we overflow
Vehicles jostling in a death dance
As weaving in and out they go.

We've paid dearly for the motor
And the 'freedom' it can bring
Gardens all turned into car parks
Pollution over everything.

As tentacles of concrete spread
Green countryside gives way to grey
And memories of gentler times
Are buried by each motorway.

Stella Hobbs

CHANGES

When I do my housework,
I think of time long past.
No mod-cons to help with the workload,
No machines to do the work fast.

I wonder at how they all managed,
how they coped with everyday chores.
Like washing their linen by hand,
and scrubbing the cold cobbled floor.

Even things have changed in my lifetime,
be it for good or for worse.
But one thing is very certain,
it's more money from out of my purse.

I wonder what it will be like,
in twenty years of more.
Will we still be hoovering the carpets,
or simply buy a new floor!

Jackie Edwards

THE ROBIN

There are footprints in the snow
A bird is in the garden, I know
there lies a feather out of a wing
When I listen I can hear him sing.
Oh, there he is, so very fat
but deary me, here comes my cat.
If he doesn't fly away quite soon,
I am certain he will meet his doom.
It is a robin so sweet and tame
I will open the door, it seems such a shame
to have to make him fly away.
At least I can say I have saved his day.

D Gilson

LOCK THEM AWAY

I have seen you stand
Behind special unbreakable windows,
Unable to see out
Whilst others look in

Banging with your fists
'Til they're swollen and sore,
Delving down for the foulest words
To express your anger and hurt,
Crying in your frustration
Shouting out your hurt
Meaning to sound *tough* and *hard*
Whilst inside,
Unlike the proverbial hedgehog,
Your heart is no longer whole.

Penny Collins

WHEN BABY COMES TO TOWN

I arrive in the world, with a hard slap on my bum,
Hanging by my heels, looking bewildered at my mum,
I don't think I deserved that, on my very first day,
Well I'll get my own back, and make that doctor pay.

I'll be on my best behaviour, while still keeping a note,
Then I'll wait until he holds me, and wet on his white coat,
It comes in quite handy, being *helpless* and small,
They'll say 'baby's had an accident', that's all.

Then I'm washed, wrapped and finally handed back to mum,
With name tag around my wrist, and something sticking out my tum,
I'll be weighed and measured, and thoroughly mucked about,
I think it's time for forty winks, now I'm really puffed out.

I don't know if I like the look, of my transparent bed,
And I have to scream the place down, just to get fed,
My nappy's changed all the time, I really don't know why,
And in front of everybody too, it's a good job I'm not shy.

Well it's my last day here, thank goodness for that,
So I'm kitted out with a matinee set, of matching boots, coat, hat . . .
As we leave the building, it's my first time outside,
Then it's into the car, for a short ride.

Once home, I meet the neighbours, who live in the street,
They make funny faces at me, and tell mum I look sweet,
I can't hear myself think, it's a jumble of voices,
And why do they stick their tongues out, and make raspberry noises?

I'll wrap adults around my little finger, in no time at all,
They'll be kept very busy, at my beck and call,
With photo album bulging, and saved for years to come,
I wonder what I'll be like, if I become a mum.

Allison Dawn Fowles

UNTITLED

'Why East Anglia?' they said.
Not only for the wide wide skies
Reminiscent of Africa,
But for the unbarred stretch
Of fields, variably coloured.
For the small villages warm
And welcoming, deep in thatch
And colour.
For towns of ancient beginnings,
Buildings and gardens echoing a rich past,
For manor houses steeped in history,
For the occasional castle ruin,
Not forbidding as in the North.
And for the great churches, magnificent
And redolent of times gone by.
But above all, for the people, welcoming,
As I was welcomed by the village post girl's greeting:
'I'm Rosie.'

Margaret Kilbey

CROATIA REVISITED

I came here to visit, a few years back,
I told myself I would return, and my footstep's track.
I admired the country, so peaceful and still,
But in so short a time, war broke out to maim and kill.

I kept my promise to myself, though people thought me mad,
I looked around and what I saw, made me oh so sad.
This beautiful country, is now hell on earth,
Only solemn, weary people, no more laughter no more mirth.

In the monastery, so remote and proud,
Peace and contentment, surround me like a shroud.
On the island of KRK, all on its own,
If only men could see, how great when love is shown.

But no! Greed is their one desire,
Guns, bombs, disaster and fire.
When will men learn and realise,
Nothing will become of this, and love will rise.

God creates and one life, is given to us,
Why can't they all live in harmony and trust.
What do they gain, with war fire and foe,
At the end what have they got to show.

A country ruined, in need of repair,
As war is evil and hate, and there is no care.
One day perhaps, they will understand,
And perhaps in peace walk hand in hand.

I have done what I have wanted to,
To visit the holy shrine, and the monastery too.
I have said my prayers at the holy shrine,
So now peace, love and contentment are surely mine.

V M Foulger

WHERE THE RIVER BENDS

The river bends in the fields near our home,
I used to fish there as a kid, all on my own,
I'd catch roach and dace and a perch here and there,
Just a boy enjoying life, not having a care.

The school holidays gave me plenty of time,
To go fishing, if the weather was fine,
I'd sit there all day, making case after cast,
All by myself and a pair of swans drifting past.

This idyllic time of youthful spring,
This flush, that only tender years can bring,
This river, like a mighty wall,
This special time, this boyhood call.

These memories of bygone time,
Of halcyon days in summertime,
Of dragonflies and sweet ozone,
Where the river bends, in the fields, near our home.

Dennis Scott

SPRINGTIME

Oh how I love the springtime
When life begins anew.
The brighter cheery mornings
And sparkling early dew.
Birds are darting here and there,
Gathering all they need
To make a comfy cosy nest,
Before they start to breed.
Stems appear above the soil,
To take upon the task
Of growing upwards every day,
Until they can unmask
The beauty of a flower.
Nature's gift for sure.
A very special time of year
I really do adore.

Yvonne Worth

FIRST WORLD WAR

Not a stick or a stone did he own.
He left his wife and his daughter at home, alone.
He thought it the right thing to do, it seemed even thrilling
To go to war and he was given a King's Shilling.

Then the reality of war became very clear.
The proud and the brave shed many a tear.
The muck, the bullets, the trenches, the stench,
The crying, the dying, English, Germans and French.

They buried the bodies right there in the mud.
Then through the ground as if they knew
For every drop of blood
A poppy grew.

E M Stevens

THE HOUSE IN THE WOOD

It stood in the autumn sunshine, the house
Still and dreaming and alone
We wondered who lived there; wished that it was ours.
Walked on, and left the house to the unknown.

The leaves were turning, all the swallows gone.
We came upon the house again,
Close enough this time to see the missing tiles
And sadly count each missing window pane.

Private had been chalked on the green door -
To keep out vandals, or keep ghosts inside?
The drive all brambled, and a rusted car,
Wild garden that had once been someone's pride.

It stood in the spring sunshine, the house -
Or rather, where the house once stood.
A lone chimney standing: bed and bath
All charred, and burnt, and tossed into the wood.

We walked around the ruin, he and I
And felt bereaved, as though it had been ours.
Thirty year old magazines, unburned, like new
Lay strewn among the wild neglected flowers.

Poor house, that wanted us to love it -
To live there - make it come alive - in vain.
In time, the wood will grow and cover it
Leave it to its dreams; we shall not come again.

E A Lamberton

THE SONG OF MANICHAEUS

I like the water from the sky
That falls into this pond so clear:
A make-believe lake all heaven and high.

I hate the water in the sea;
It tastes just like a human tear,
A silver, splashing stream washing o'er me.

This estuary, is where I always swim
Never straying away too far,
Not tempted by the upstream hymn
Singing with an effervescent charm,
Nor gliding out to the waves and stars
Where I'm bound to sing a drowning psalm;
Instead, happy to paddle and splash
Avoiding the lightning floods that flash,
Crashing down so soon after the calm.

No, I'm no Noah;
I have no ark
To sail way with a dark smile.
I'm not an Ararat
Rising above the waves
Singing praise in the morning light all mild.

I love the water from the sky
That fills up this pond so clear:
Yet it's only light I love and darkness that I fear.

Julian Pack

RULES, RULES, RULES

If you keep me nice and tidy
Saturday, Sunday, through to Friday
You'll still get your pocket money,
'Cos looking a mess, it isn't funny.

Pick your clothes up from the floor
Or I won't wash them any more
Don't put clean clothes in the bin.
You've got a wardrobe to hang them in.

Old cups, dirty plates, you must be joking.
How can we ever invite folk in.
Crusty cheese sarnies from the day before last.
Being untidy is now a thing of the past.

So don't be difficult, do as I say.
Make your bed and tidy up day by day.
So keep your mother happy, don't let me down.
Or I am going to have a
        Nervous breakdown!

Ellen Emptage

MEN WITHOUT DOGS

Men without dogs, never in pairs.
Salesmen at lunch, not selling their wares.
Parked in their cars or strolling about,
a cause for concern? A shadow of doubt? . . .

Walking with dogs in the calm of the morning,
they sense an approach, you are given a warning.
At first you just hear the labour of breathing,
then turning around, a jogger appearing.

Strolling at night it's just turning dark,
peering around, the dogs start to bark.
Calling them close keeping them near,
you step up the pace, ears strained to hear.

Women with dogs out in all weather
these men without dogs, we lump them together.
How can you tell, how can you know
which ones to fear, how does it show.

Us women with dogs we all wear the same.
Trainers or wellies, we know the game.
Sweat pants or jeans an old anorak,
no sexual allure in that tatty old mac.

We dress down and walk alone every day
except for our dogs, we like it that way.
But every so often like a whisper of fate
we're a moment too early, or a moment too late.

Do these men without dogs who wander about
causing alarm, suspicion and doubt,
Do they ever consider the fear they create
walking about, or sitting in wait.

Barbara Puddyford

STANSTEAD AIRPORT

Stansted Airport I watched it grow
From fields my grandad used to sow
He was the first to sell his land
And that is how it all began.

In '42 with great haste
The Yanks came, no time waste
Hitler was getting the upper hand
They came to help defend our land

Marauders huge filled the sky
Not all came back, some had to die
But in the end Hitler was defeated
The Yanks left, their mission completed.

After the war planes still flew
Until it was decided then we knew
London's third airport it was to be
So again I was to see

Diggers, cranes and men come again
Oh! The mud with so much rain
Houses flattened, roads redirected
As a new terminal was erected.

A beautiful building of perfection
At night gives off a warm reflection
In the sky you see it shine
A symbol of a better time.

M Barker

UNTITLED

The daffodils are blooming and the sun is shining bright
The garden is awakening - it is a wondrous sight
The buds are bursting everywhere, the crocuses are out
The blossom on the cherry trees makes me want to shout
The dark brown earth is giving up its secrets from below
And all around the bird song sounds are making sure we know
That winter's almost over now and days are lengthening
The summer sun will warm us soon, the air smells sweet with spring.

Jacqueline Heatnett

NO MATTER . . .

Can you still get up with ease -
No matter how many times you are knocked down?
Can you hide your wounded pride
And brush aspersions to one side,
Denying all the hurts inside
With the illusion of a clown?

Can you still find room for love -
No matter how many times your heart is broken?
Can you search for love again
Through disappointments and the pain,
When it seems to be in vain
To end in harsh words plainly spoken?

Can you still depend on friends -
No matter how many times you've been forsaken?
Can you count on many hands
Or do they slide like silken strands
Or blow away like shifting sands
And once again you are mistaken?

Can you still pursue your dreams -
No matter how many dreams may lie in tatters?
Can you strive for dreams anew
And carry on like dreamers do
Until the day it dawns on you
That happiness is all that matters.

But, no matter . . .

Blaby Little

DREAMS

I've travelled the world in my dreams
So many places have I seen
The Middle East so full of spice
France with its wine so fine
And restaurants with food so sublime
The mysteries of the world have unfolded before me
So many different people leading such different lives
Poverty starvation wealth and thrive
You can't live your own without touching another
We all have to rely on each other
The sights of the world will be with me forever
People with fear and hate in their faces
Airports full of travellers with suitcases
Cities with no open spaces
My dreams are nothing like that at all
People smile some even talk
In the cities at night you can walk
Gentle music is in the air
And birds fly past ducking here and there
Wait I hear the bells a calling
Oh well it must now be morning.

D Allen

DESTITUTION

Accommodation for the nation
doesn't match our expectations.
The youth revolt and start to moan
but politicians ignore our raging tone.
Roaming the streets scrounging for food,
the neglected homeless are silently booed.
Wasting our days begging for credit,
our future looks bleak; we've almost had it.
The average man only turns his back,
treating the abandoned like a verminous rat.
Avoiding the subways, he doesn't think twice,
survival for us is like a game of dice.
Nobody cares if we become skin and bones
as we're as welcome as the sight of motorway cones.

Surely someone can spare us a roof
or else it's kipping again in a phone booth.
As our parents have given us a rough deal,
now we must steal to pay for a meal.
If we'd been encouraged while still at school
perhaps we wouldn't be falling off this wobbly stool.
We have no abode, so we can't claim benefit;
there isn't a doubt the system's screwing us bit by bit.
What chance have we of getting a job
when we are just seen as shameless yobs?
People should never judge our intelligence
on the fact that we only have a few pence.
Give us a glimmer of hope to cling to,
please make it soon, before we are through!

Tay Collicutt

FOTHERINGHAY

As the mists of time fade away,
I'm going back to Fotheringhay.
My captive queen in an alien land,
Awaiting release by a violent hand.
As the mists of time fade away,
I have returned to Fotheringhay.
Once the young Queen of an exciting land,
With Francis to spend her life she had planned.
As the mists of time fade away,
I see her cry at Fotheringhay.
On her last night she remembers her life,
Twice a queen, three times a wife.
As the mists of time fade away,
I hear her sigh at Fotheringhay.
The hammers stop, the work is done,
The scaffold is ready for a royal one.
As the mists of time fade away,
Her ladies weep at Fotheringhay.
The morning comes and she prepares to go,
She feels at peace, no more sorrow.
As the mists of time fade away,
Her head's held high at Fotheringhay.
Her beauty's gone, her joints, in pain,
She's helped to the room she'll never see again.
As the mists of time roll away,
A hush falls upon Fotheringhay.
The scaffold awaits, she steps up,
Her head is severed at the third cut.
And as the mists of time fade away,
They kill my Queen at Fotheringhay.

Lynda Miller

THE RECOVERY PARTY

We left him there despite recognising his plea
'Bitte helfen Sie mir, um Himmels Willen,
Bitte helfen Sie mir'
For we had our own to haul in before dawn's curfew.

But going past again, humanity overcame.
His empty pistol - we loaded one chamber
And knowingly wrapped his weak grip.

A relief broke through the twisted grimace
And thanks were offered, for rest was promised.
Surely those next minutes were like hours
Until we heard the endless misery was likely ended.

John Kemp

DRIFTING AWAY

I lay on my bed and drift away
to another land another day
The sky was green, the land was blue
in this land I met you
You showed me all kinds of things
like a great bird with beautiful wings
Cats and dogs living in the sea
all these things are strange to me
All the fish live on the lands
and the people walk on their hands
I looked up in the sky
strange things were flying by
Suddenly one touched my brow
I woke up! Where am I now?
The dream was gone, lost in my head
I suppose I'd better get out of bed.

A Ingram

LILIES AND CLOUDS

Something old, something new
Something borrowed, something blue,
But white is the wedding gown.
Something battered something bruised,
Something soiled, something used,
But white are lilies and clouds.

But fear becomes fact
And white becomes black,
As veils turn to shrouds,
Ashes to ashes, dust to dust.
Over time a cheap ring will rust,
But white are lilies and clouds.

Toby North

TWO LIVES, ONE JOURNEY

At the altar in unity it began,
So far 'tis of a forty-year span!
Having left the altar
Unto us two of son and
Two of daughter.

We travelled far in different lands,
O'er mighty seas, through changing skies . . .
Sometimes we walked
Through fields of clover;
At others we traversed paths
Where all was clouded over, with atmosphere frosty -
Cold enough for snow. Tempests tossed us
On rough seas . . . but all eventually abated
And rays of sun elated.

When he - or me - dies,
It will not be *he* or *me*
But *we* who have died.
Then the journey will be over;
Then, there will be no more clover.

Doreen McGee-Osborne

METAMORPHOSIS

Emerging from chrysalis, beautiful butterfly,
Giving great pleasure to all who pass by;
Brilliant colours invade the sky.
Dazzle the earth with your colourful hue,
Feasting on flowers that camouflage you.

Fluttering here and fluttering there,
Apparently your predators seem quite unaware, as you
Carefully deposit your eggs from their view,
Eventually, caterpillars will replace you!

R A Kemp

SWEET 16

I look in the mirror,
tell you what I see,
eyes, nose, cheeks and mouth,
smiling back, oh so pretty.
A beautiful face,
Scarred by life,
A beautiful face,
Up soon for sacrifice.

Look at me slowly,
look at me quick.
Keep mind of my face,
as my soul will make you sick.
Pretty as I am,
this world I have to face,
no time have I to enjoy
my only saving grace.

This world lies in front of me,
and I don't know how to use it,
do I bounce it like a ball,
or throw it like a frisbee.
At 17 I'll start to decline,
What fun have I had,
What fun was due?
The act I must follow,
will come too soon.

Sweet 16
and what's it worth.
A bullet in the heart
and a mind full of dirt.

Aysha Vanderman

FENLAND HOME

Turquoise sky with powder puffs of white -
Brilliant light as far as you can see;
Pale green and gold and cream and ivory.

A tinge of pink above, a dark green hedge,
Among the flaxen wheat the poppies red.
Then sparkling in the distance silvery,
the River Ouse flows gently out to sea.
The fertile fields tilled by the Fenman's hand
Produce in plenty food and sustenance.

Historic towns and villages, cathedrals, Stately homes,
The churches with their Anglo Saxon - Norman spires and domes.

The wild fowl on the river banks, of the Ouse the Nene and Cam;
The stately rushes by canals that are there to drain the land.
Patchwork meadows, winding roads deep ditches either side.
The view that unfolds before your eyes isn't so much land - more sky.
Some say the fenland scene is stark and flat
But I cannot agree with that.
The beauty of the land is clear to me.
If you have perceptive eye you'll see the colours, lights and shades,
the sweeps, the lines, the living hedgerows from Mediaeval times.

In many parts it seems that time's stood still
With mellow brick and thatch and village pond
with ducks and geese or moorhens swimming on.
Most counties of the island I have seen
and each of them for me has had its charm
But the fenlands of my ancestors here before recorded time
is where I wish to pass my days and live my allotted time.

Doris L Ward

FEN MUSE

It's boring to me
there's nothing to see.
There's a beautiful sky.

It's incredibly flat,
what made it like that?
Look at the sky.

The fields are so low
T'was Vermuyden you know
who uncovered the sky.

He drained all the peat,
an incredible feat,
and there was the sky.

The peat is now drying,
with the wind it is flying,
a darkening sky.

Look that's a peat blow.
It looks like brown snow,
I can't see the sky.

A bog oak you say?
From millennia away,
it once reached the sky.

I quite like it here,
there's a great atmosphere,
and a bcautiful sky.

Helen Samuels

HISTORY REVISITED

Down to St Ives went my sister and me,
St Nick and his reindeer we had hoped to see;
He came in by boat - seven reindeer propulsion -
To switch on Christmas lights, a festive commotion.
Each reindeer, it seems, had seven sacks 'round his neck,
Each sack seven elves, each elf seven pecks,
Each peck was made up of mince pies, sweets and toys
To delight all the mums, dads, girls and small boys.
My sister and I, we had the same question,
How many, we wondered, had a St Ives destination?

Sharyl K Honstein

THE SWASTIKA

Oh . . . swastika thou crooked cross foul, symbol of a nation's loss.
Of its human dignity.
Born of perverted twisted brains creeping like cancer in the hearts of men
turning their minds to black iniquity.
See. From thine evil shrine dark figures rise. The murdered innocents
whose ghastly cries.
You spurned . . . when drunk with Teutonic lust for power.
You herded them like sheep en-masse. To the slaughter and the gas.
See how now with ghostly hands. They point at you and in the van
six million.
Each one a Jew.
The world remembering bows its head in shame
For swastika thou hast made it plain. So very plain.
That man's destiny far from being in a twinkling star.
His future could end in atomic war.
Unless by using his one saving skill. The exercise of his own free will.
He turns again with humble grace and with God's truth does humbly face.
That the brain like the body passes away Nor is God's own image shaped in
our human clay.
For it is the soul that lives within us that forms the perfect part.
The true and godly image that links the human heart.
With Creation's glory from which all life on earth began
And when all life on earth is ended to which it must return.

J S Reid

THE OLD WOMAN

Now by the fire you sit, your long day over,
Dreaming perhaps of youth, of friend and lover,
Husband and children, health and strength and daring,
Lost in the mists of time, the years of caring.
Thinking sometimes of duty bravely done,
Of battles sometimes, sometimes victories won.
In quiet content that, if this life be ended,
There waits another, luminous, vast and splendid.

Eileen Watkins

ESSEX SUMMER

Essex lanes are brimming
Now with seas of cream and green;
Queen Anne's lace and meadow sweet,
Hawthorn white and wild rose pink,
Suffuse this fairest scene.

Town fetes and village fairs teem
With myriad stalls - cakes, jam and flowers
Stacks of books and mounds of bric-a-brac.
Merry games and furious fun burst
From Flitch, Morris, seaside and castle towers.

Our history shines through roads and homes
In names from ancient days;
Epping, Roding, Mistley, Colchester and Grays.
Sunlit Saffron pargetting views with golden thatch,
While over all church steeples call to eternal ways.

Patricia March

NO PAIN, NO GAIN

Twist his feet, they say
Turn them harder, this way
Just a baby, my baby
Soft, blue unfocussed eyes
Demanding love, trusting me.
Me twisting, you writhing
Me turning, stomach churning
You crying, tiny hands flailing
Red face contorting.
Oh God, this is hurting
Am I doing this right?
Twist his feet, they say
Turn them harder, this way.
Will he walk, will he run?
My child, my son
Both of us crying quiet tears
Mouthing silent screams.
Grit my teeth, grab his foot
Start twisting again.
No gain without pain
Turn them harder, they say.
This goes against nature
This thing I must do.
I do it for love
I do it for you
My poor clubfooted boy.

Barbara Prager

AN ENGLISH SUMMER

Two weeks in Norfolk with so much to see
Cromer and Hemsby and Wells-next-the-Sea
Cathedral in Norwich, museums in Kings Lynn
A boat on the Broads - try not to fall in!

Day trips to Yarmouth and Caister-on-Sea
Mummy and Daddy, my brother and me
Shrimp nets and windmills, buckets and spades
Swimsuits and sandals, sunhats and sunshades

Feeding the seagulls that shrieked up on high
Or searching for crabs which were left high and dry
Seaweed all slimy and stones that hurt feet
Donkeys with hats on to shade from the heat

Freezing cold water that took breath away
Running from waves, getting soaked by the spray
A beautiful sandcastle but, oh, how we cried
When we watched as it fell, washed away by the tide!

Wrestling with deckchairs that had minds of their own
There was always a wasp that wouldn't leave you alone
Punch and Judy and strawberry ice cream
Candyfloss, rock, a small child's dream.

Hampers of sandwiches, flasks full of tea
Don't you recall your days by the sea?
Collecting seashells along the seashore
Nostalgic reminders of childhood of yore.

Vacations in England, caravan in tow
We've had gales and hailstorms but never yet snow
We could have visited Spain or seen Gay Paris
But the South-East of England is just fine by me.

A Edwards

UNDER LOCK AND KEY

There is so much to do and view
This county is a hit
But there's a spot in Cambridgeshire
That few wish to visit.
It lies near Grafham Water
By the village of Perry
And it has been my residence
Since summer '93.
It's called H M P Littlehey
Your board and lodgings free
But you are charged to come here
Then you're under lock and key
There's bars but they do not sell beer
A human zoo, the public fear
And when the keepers close the gate
The turning key will seal our fate.
Yes Cambridgeshire's a lovely place
To explore any day
But keep your nose clean
Or you might end up in Littlehey!

Roger Carpenter

UNTITLED

The essence of life,
Tall, slender reaches.
Silhouetted against
Blue, grey and even red.
Almost eternal
Power to give life
Yet not protect it.
Destruction equals end,
Desertification of life.
So simple, calm
From amber to emerald
Every time, no fail.
Unless wrenched,
Tugged from life's roots.
Thoughtlessness
Loses the creator and . . .
Eventually the created too.

J L Knight (16)

NORFOLK

Reed and knapped flint, these are our Norfolk bounty,
The one, sturdy and tenacious despite the East wind's salty surge,
Like our stubborn nature that 'all us keep a-doin', bor', whatever comes,
The other, broad, flat, dependable as the vowels we inherit
From those whose secret dust enriches all our eastward earth.

Under our wide, our ever-changing yet abiding sky,
The centuries have shaped our towns, our villages,
Carved out our lokes, our highways, broad, marsh and mead.
Legionaries, sighing for their golden sunny land
Stared in despair across the grey marsh mornings,
Yet knew the subtle magic of this most secret world.
Rumbustious Danes, surging up our empty, wind-swept beaches,
Left more lasting mark than melting footprints on the sand.

More invaders. And yet more. But our rich ground
Received them all, shaped them with her ancient power
And forged a resolute breed, slow of speech, deep of heart,
Blessed with dry humour like fleeting sun on their un-hurried rivers.

We are a privileged people, we, the North-folk born and bred,
Whose heritage of soaring spire, of peerless lonely churches
Is more, far more, than merely charming landscape,
Meriting poem, painting, song . . . we share a majesty.

Audrey Capp-Serreau

INFORMATION

We hope you have enjoyed reading this book - and that you will continue to enjoy it in the coming years.

If you like reading and writing poetry drop us a line, or give us a call, and we'll send you a free information pack.

Write to

Anchor Books Information
1-2 Wainman Road
Woodston
Peterborough
PE2 7BU.